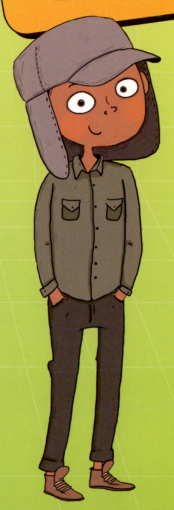

A Benjamin Blog
and his Inquisitive Dog
Investigation

Exploring Deserts

Anita Ganeri

Heinemann
LIBRARY

Chicago, Illinois

© 2014 Heinemann Library
an imprint of Capstone Global Library, LLC
Chicago, Illinois

To contact Capstone Global Library please
phone 800-747-4992, or visit our web site,
www.capstonepub.com

Edited by Dan Nunn, Rebecca Rissman, and Helen
Cox Cannons
Designed by Joanna Hinton-Malivoire
Original illustrations © Capstone Global Library Ltd
Illustrated by Sernur ISIK
Picture research by Mica Brancic
Production by Helen McCreath
Originated by Capstone Global Library Ltd
Printed and bound in China

17 16 15 14 13
10 9 8 7 6 5 4 3 2 1

**Library of Congress Cataloging-in-Publication
Data**
Ganeri, Anita, 1961- author.
  Exploring deserts : a Benjamin Blog and his
inquisitive dog investigation / Anita Ganeri.
    pages cm.—(Exploring habitats, with Benjamin
Blog and his inquisitive dog)
  Includes bibliographical references and index.
  ISBN 978-1-4329-8778-7 (hb)—ISBN 978-1-4329-
8785-5 (pb) 1. Desert ecology—Juvenile literature.
2. Deserts—Juvenile literature. 3. Desert animals—
Juvenile literature. I. Title.

QH541.5.D4G36 2014
551.41′5—dc23   2013017415

Acknowledgments
The author and publisher are grateful to the
following for permission to reproduce copyright
material: Alamy p. 26 (© Joerg Boethling);
Corbis pp. 10 (© John Carnemolla), 27
(George Steinmetz); FLPA p. 15 (Imagebroker/
Michael Weber); Getty Images pp . 17 (Stone/©
Paul Chesley), 18 (Universal Images Group/
Auscape), Photoshot p. 16 (© NHPA/Alberto
Nardi); Shutterstock pp. 4 (© Galyna Andrushko),
6 (© somchaij), 7 (© Yoann Combronde), 9
(© Denis Burdin), 11 (© Tom Grundy), 12 (©
Maxim Petrichuk), 13 (© pixy), 14 (© Isabella
Pfenninger), 19 (© joyfull), 21 (© angelo lano), 23
(© Joao Virissimo), 29 top (© nito), 29 bottom (©
azhuvalappil); SuperStock pp. 5 (imagebroker.
net/Michael Weber), 8 (age footstock), 20
(Robert Harding Picture Library), 22 (Tier und
Naturfotografie), 24 (imagebroker.net/Egmont
Strigl), 25 (Mauritius/Frank Lukasseck).

Cover photograph of the Sahara Desert, Algeria,
reproduced with permission of Shutterstock (©
Pichugin Dmitry).

We would like to thank Michael Bright for his
invaluable help in the preparation of this book.

Every effort has been made to contact copyright
holders of any material reproduced in this book.
Any omissions will be rectified in subsequent
printings if notice is given to the publisher.

All the Internet addresses (URLs) given in this
book were valid at the time of going to press.
However, due to the dynamic nature of the
Internet, some addresses may have changed,
or sites may have changed or ceased to exist
since publication. While the author and publisher
regret any inconvenience this may cause readers,
no responsibility for any such changes can be
accepted by either the author or the publisher.

Some words are shown in bold, **like this**. You can find
out what they mean by looking in the glossary.

Contents

Welcome to the Desert!

Hello! My name's Benjamin Blog and this is Barko Polo, my **inquisitive** dog. (He's named after the ancient ace explorer **Marco Polo**.) We have just returned from our latest adventure— exploring **deserts** around the world. We put this book together from some of the blog posts we wrote on the way.

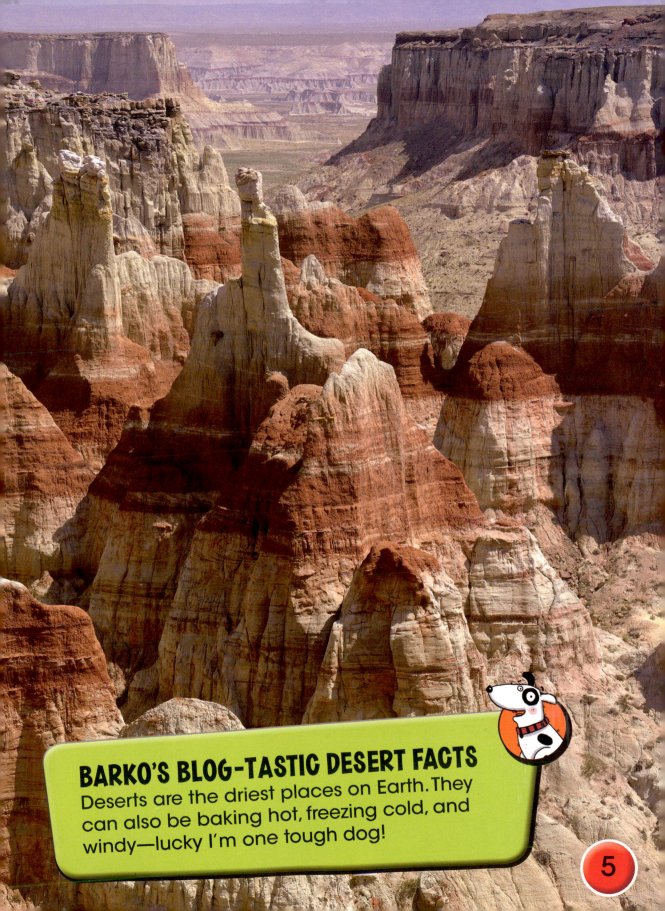

BARKO'S BLOG-TASTIC DESERT FACTS

Deserts are the driest places on Earth. They can also be baking hot, freezing cold, and windy—lucky I'm one tough dog!

What a Scorcher

Posted by: Ben Blog | April 16 at 10:48 a.m.

Here we are in the Sahara **Desert** in north Africa, and it's seriously hot. This deadly desert can reach a scorching 122 degrees Fahrenheit (50 degrees Celsius) in the daytime, though it's much cooler at night. Phew! Other deserts, like the Gobi in China and Mongolia, are warm in summer but bitterly cold in the winter.

BARKO'S BLOG-TASTIC DESERT FACTS

Deserts are as dry as a bone because they hardly get any rain. In parts of the Atacama Desert in Chile, it hasn't rained at all for hundreds of years. Yikes!

Sand Everywhere

Posted by: Ben Blog | May 9 at 12:06 p.m.

The first thing we noticed about the Arabian **Desert** is the sand. It gets everywhere! The particular part of the desert in this photo is called the Rub al-Khali (which means "Empty Quarter"). It's the world's biggest **sand sea**—bigger than the country of France.

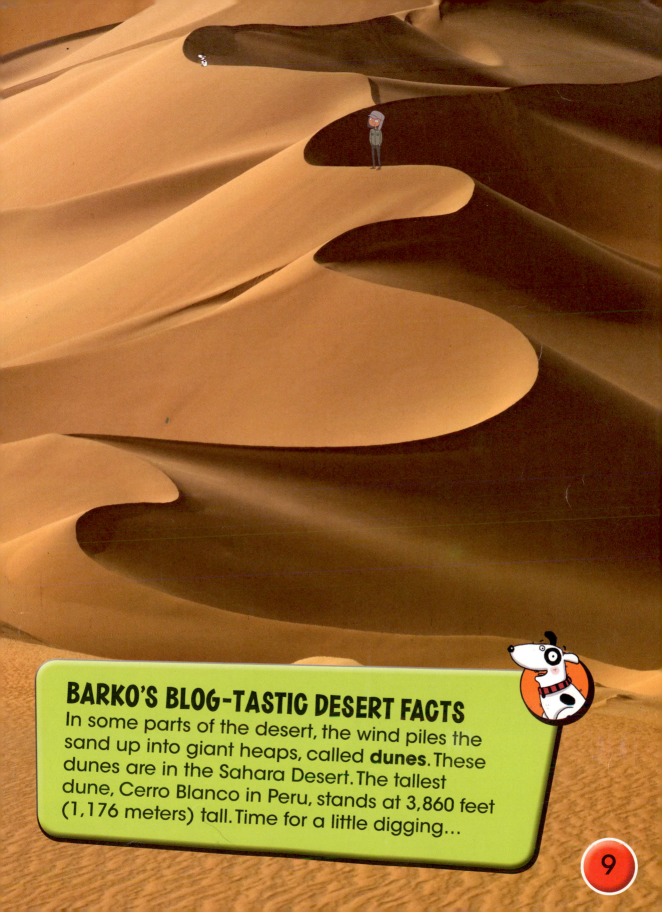

BARKO'S BLOG-TASTIC DESERT FACTS

In some parts of the desert, the wind piles the sand up into giant heaps, called **dunes**. These dunes are in the Sahara Desert. The tallest dune, Cerro Blanco in Peru, stands at 3,860 feet (1,176 meters) tall. Time for a little digging…

Stone, Rock, and Salt

Posted by: Ben Blog | June 24 at 2:35 p.m.

I used to think that all **deserts** were sandy until I saw this place. It is the Sturt Stony Desert in Australia, and it is covered in masses of small, red rocks and stones. In fact, most deserts are rocky or stony, not sandy. Some are even covered in salt!

BARKO'S BLOG-TASTIC DESERT FACTS

Playas are flat, salty **plains** in the desert. They are formed from dried-up **salt lakes**. This one is in the Mojave Desert in the southwest United States.

Caught in a Storm

Posted by: Ben Blog | July 13 at 11:27 a.m.

We're exploring the **desert** in Kazakhstan. We got stuck in a sandstorm. It was so fierce that we could hardly see a thing. In a sandstorm, the wind races across the ground, whipping up the sand. You can't breathe very well, and the sand stings your skin.

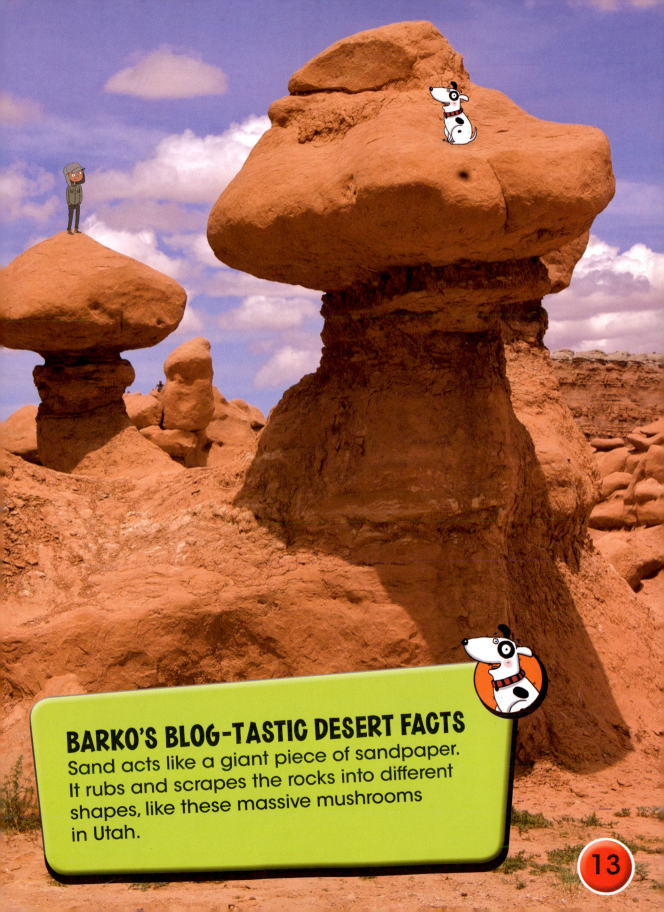

BARKO'S BLOG-TASTIC DESERT FACTS

Sand acts like a giant piece of sandpaper. It rubs and scrapes the rocks into different shapes, like these massive mushrooms in Utah.

Getting into a Scrape

Sand is not the only thing that shapes the **desert**. Check out this photo I took of a deep valley called a **wadi**. When it rains, water rushes along it, carrying along stones and pebbles, which scrape and scour the rocks.

We are here.

BARKO'S BLOG-TASTIC DESERT FACTS

Mesas are huge, flat-topped mountains in the desert. They are left behind when the land around them is worn away by the wind and rain. *Mesa* means "table" in Spanish.

Cool Characters

Posted by: Ben Blog | September 20 at 4:43 p.m.

We met some amazing animals on our travels. I managed to take a photo of this little fennec fox in the Sahara. It's a really cool character. Its huge ears aren't just useful for listening for **gerbils** and other **prey**. They also lose lots of heat to keep the fox's body cool.

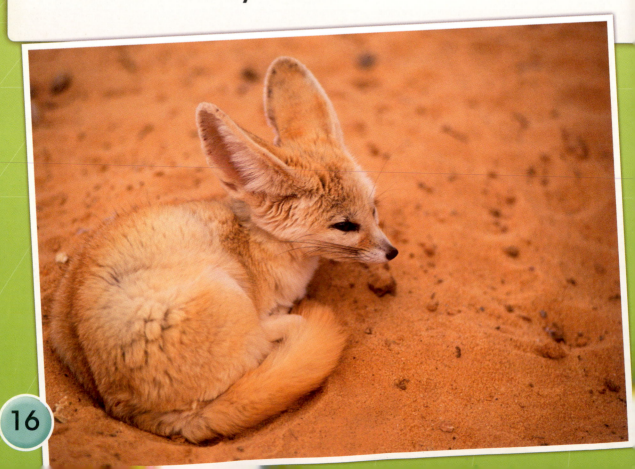

BARKO'S BLOG-TASTIC DESERT FACTS
A sidewinder snake moves by flipping its body sideways. That way, it only needs to touch the hot sand for a few seconds. I think I'll try it…

Another problem that **desert** animals have to face is getting enough water. In dry weather, the water-holding frog from Australia finds shelter in a damp burrow underground. It wraps its body in slime to stop it from drying out and stores water in pockets under its skin.

BARKO'S BLOG-TASTIC DESERT FACTS

Camels can survive for weeks without eating.
Instead, they live off fat stored in their humps.
They can also go for days without drinking.
But exploring the desert is thirsty work for dogs!

Blooming Desert

Posted by: Ben Blog | October 9 at 1:09 p.m.

Like animals, plants need water to survive. But where do **desert** plants find a drink? I came across this weird-looking plant in the Namib Desert in Namibia. It's called a welwitschia. It uses its long, **frayed** leaves to collect tiny droplets of fog that blow in from the ocean.

BARKO'S BLOG-TASTIC DESERT FACTS

The baobab tree from Madagascar and South Africa has a huge trunk that fills up with water and swells. It's also called the upside-down tree because it looks as if its roots are sticking out of the top.

Remember the Sturt Stony Desert in Australia? I spotted these Sturt's desert peas while we were there. Their seeds lie in the ground for many months until it rains. Then they sprout and bloom very quickly before the desert dries up again.

BARKO'S BLOG-TASTIC DESERT FACTS

Giant saguaro cacti grow in the United States. They have different ways of saving water. They store water in their stems, and their sharp spines don't lose as much water as leaves. Ouch!

Super Sahara

Posted by: Ben Blog | November 11 at 11:59 a.m.

We are back in the Sahara—my favorite desert on Earth. It's also the world's biggest desert. It's larger than the continent of Australia. Amazingly, thousands of years ago, the Sahara was lush and green. These are some ancient cave paintings of an elephant and giraffes that lived there.

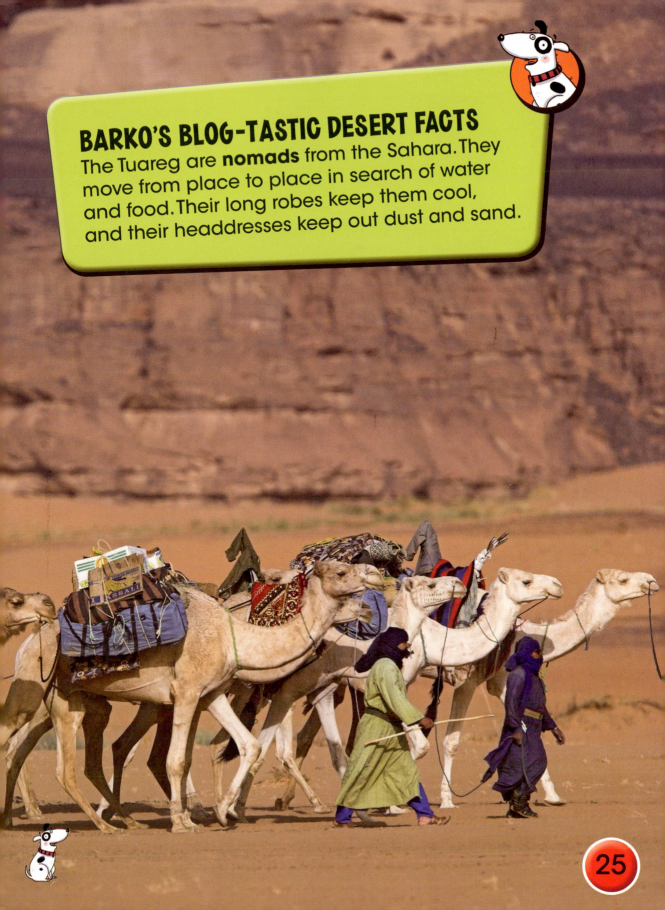

BARKO'S BLOG-TASTIC DESERT FACTS

The Tuareg are **nomads** from the Sahara. They move from place to place in search of water and food. Their long robes keep them cool, and their headdresses keep out dust and sand.

Danger: Desert Spread

Posted by: Ben Blog | December 13 at 2:32 p.m.

All over the world, **deserts** are spreading. People are cutting down too many trees for firewood and clearing too much land for farming. This is the Sahel on the edge of the Sahara. It's turning to dust, which is not good for growing crops.

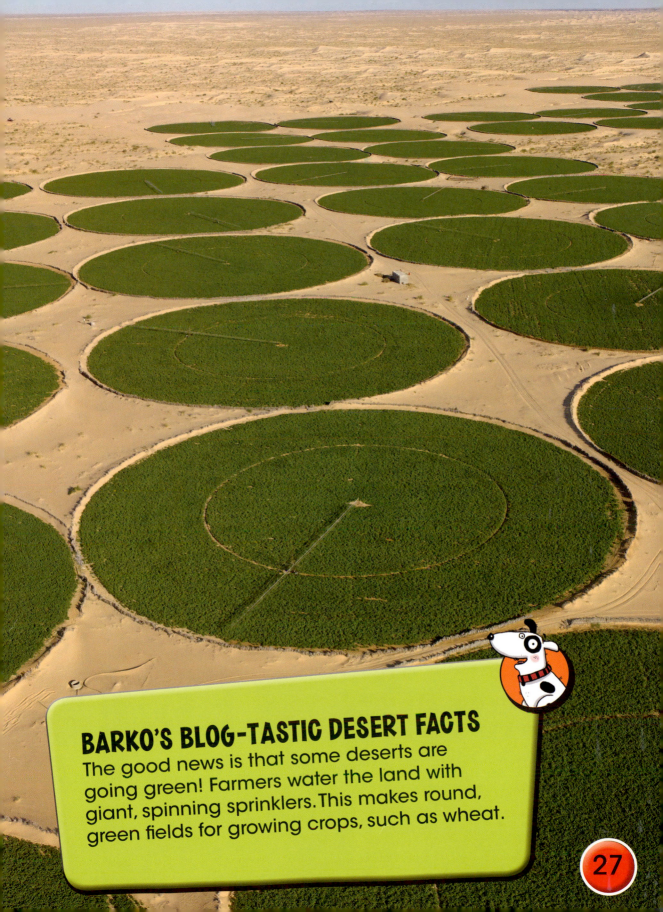

BARKO'S BLOG-TASTIC DESERT FACTS
The good news is that some deserts are going green! Farmers water the land with giant, spinning sprinklers. This makes round, green fields for growing crops, such as wheat.

Deadly Deserts Quiz

If you are planning your own **desert** expedition, you need to be prepared. Find out how much you know about deadly deserts with our quick quiz.

1. Which is the biggest desert?
a) Gobi
b) Sturt Stony
c) Sahara

2. Where is the driest desert?
a) Chile
b) Australia
c) Africa

3. What causes a sandstorm?
a) wind
b) rain
c) cold

4. What is a **mesa**?
a) a pile of sand
b) a flat-topped mountain
c) a groove in the rock

5. How do sidewinders move?
a) by jumping
b) by hopping
c) by flipping sideways

6. What do baobabs store in their trunks?
a) water
b) honey
c) nuts

7. What is this?

8. What is this?

Glossary

desert place that is extremely dry because it gets very little rain

dune giant heap of sand, piled up by the wind

frayed with torn or ragged edges

gerbil mouse-like desert creature, with long back legs

inquisitive interested in learning about the world

Marco Polo explorer who lived from about 1254 to 1324. He traveled from Italy to China.

mesa huge, flat-topped mountain in the desert

nomad person who moves from place to place to find food and water

plain large, flat stretch of land

playas flat, salty plains in the desert

prey animals that are hunted and eaten by other animals

salt lake lake that is filled with salty water

sand sea huge area of sand in a desert

wadi deep valley in the desert that fills with water when it rains

Find Out More

Books

Ganeri, Anita. *Harsh Habitats.* Chicago: Raintree, 2013.

Gray, Leon. *Deserts* (Geography Wise). New York: Rosen, 2011.

Murphy, Julie. *Desert Animal Adaptations.* Mankato, Minn.: Capstone, 2012.

Underwood, Deborah. *Hiding in Deserts.* Chicago: Heinemann, 2011.

Web Sites

FactHound offers a safe, fun way to find Internet sites related to this book. All of the sites on FactHound have been researched by our staff.

Here's all you do:
Visit www.facthound.com
Type in this code: 9781432987787

Index